JAMES

C000185279

FOOTBALLERS'
Haircuts
A NEW HISTORY

WEIDENFELD & NICOLSON

TRIFON IVANOV

Introduction

Forget the '60s. Don't even think about the '70s. And as for the '80s – well, that's ancient history. It wasn't just footballers who had funny haircuts way back then – everybody did.

The last twenty years have been a new golden age of footballers' haircuts and we'll look back upon them with the same mix of fondness and disbelief that their illustrious forefathers were regarded with.

From those that let it all get too long, to those who spend every afternoon in the salon – the mohicans, the dreadlocks and all the colours of the rainbow... we celebrate them all.

David Beckham

The mohican, the skinhead, the beard, the floppy fringed schoolboy – David Beckham has had them all. He is the king of footballers' haircuts – although we're sure he'd make the distinction between a haircut and a hairstyle.

He epitomises the showbiz aspect of football, where image is everything. His legacy may well be the reinvention of the footballers' haircut – for without his influence football haircuts would be stuck in the past.

Beckham is certainly a style icon. Where he leads others inevitably follow, but he's always the first and always the best. The only 'style' he hasn't tried is the Chris Waddle mullet – but if anyone could, and he probably will, it's him.

2002

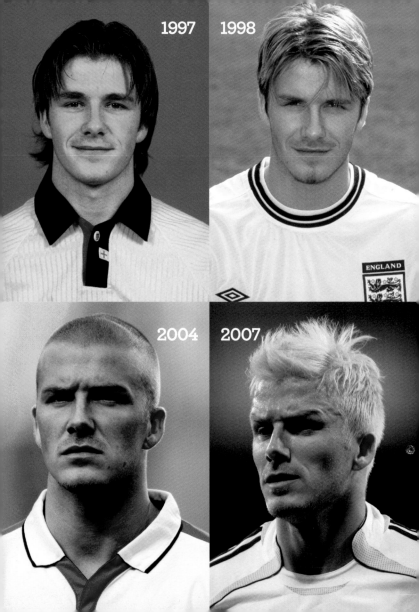

Seventies Throwbacks

When people say 'footballers' haircut', what first springs to mind are those halcyon days of the '70s – the unholy trinity of Kevin Keegan, Gerry Francis and Charlie George. Nowadays, if a player grows his hair long, there's always going to be a touch of the '70s about him. You can't look at Robbie Savage without thinking of Brut 33.

Long hair whether straight or curly is definitely a 'Haircut' not a 'Hairstyle', no-nonsense and carefree. It's most commonly seen on a creative maverick-type midfielder or a ball playing centreback. Some nations are more prone to the '70s haircut than others – 90% of the 2010 Argentine World Cup squad drew their inspiration from the great 1978 side.

RAY PARLOUR

RAY OF LIGHT

Forget the 'Romford Pele' nickname, with his ginger ringlets Parlour was more 'Romford Keegan'. Before the 1998 World Cup he asked Glenn Hoddle's spiritual healer Eileen Drury for a short back and sides, after which he never played for England again.

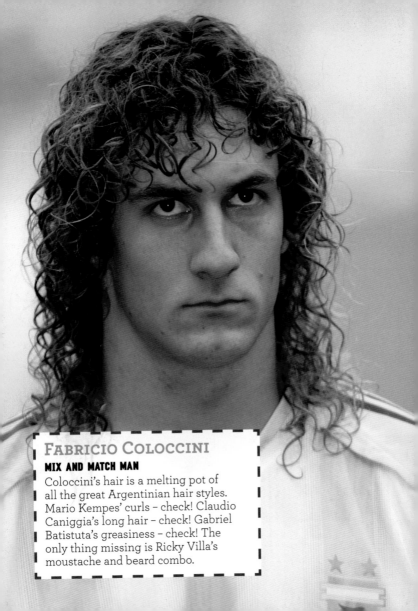

FABRICIO COLOCCINI

MIX AND MATCH MAN

Coloccini's hair is a melting pot of all the great Argentinian hair styles. Mario Kempes' curls – check! Claudio Caniggia's long hair – check! Gabriel Batistuta's greasiness – check! The only thing missing is Ricky Villa's moustache and beard combo.

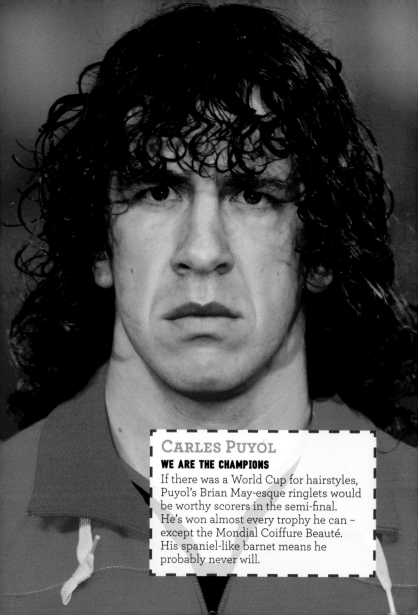

CARLES PUYOL

WE ARE THE CHAMPIONS

If there was a World Cup for hairstyles,
Puyol's Brian May-esque ringlets would
be worthy scorers in the semi-final.
He's won almost every trophy he can –
except the Mondial Coiffure Beauté.
His spaniel-like barnet means he
probably never will.

TIM SHERWOOD

KINKY AFRO

It's hard to believe that in 1995, when Sherwood won the league with Blackburn, a 'Happy Mondays' haircut like his was considered stylish and was relatively common.

ROBBIE SAVAGE
THE HAIR & THE TEETH & THE TAN
Universally derided for being too flash, his Essex housewife hair was a bit too feminine for the hard man image he got saddled with.

JONATHAN WOODGATE

JOHNNY B GOODE

Woodgate's bad luck with injuries means that he has had plenty of time to grow his hair in the treatment room. So much so that he's perfected the Point Break surfer look. Like, totally awesome, dude.

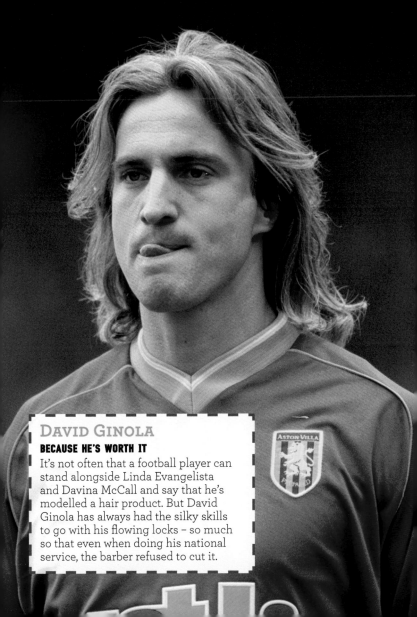

DAVID GINOLA

BECAUSE HE'S WORTH IT

It's not often that a football player can stand alongside Linda Evangelista and Davina McCall and say that he's modelled a hair product. But David Ginola has always had the silky skills to go with his flowing locks – so much so that even when doing his national service, the barber refused to cut it.

Headbands

There are those players who like a little more discipline to their long hair. They choose the headband. Whether it is as thin as a piece of cotton or so wide that it looks more like a hat, it's safe to say that it's the modern-day equivalent of the mullet. The headband is for players who want the rebelliousness of long hair but without any of the hassle of it getting in their eyes.

A lot of footballers' haircuts have passed into public use but you don't see many men out on the town wearing a headband. It's called an Alice band for a reason.

And of course when it all gets a bit too long, the headband gets a little smaller and you are in the far dodgier territory of the ponytail.

GIANLUIGI BUFFON

THANK HEAVEN FOR GIGI

Buffon's hair isn't that long but clearly
he's a man who doesn't like it in his eyes.
He takes the headband to new lengths
(or widths) - it looks like he has gaffer
taped his hair into place - or maybe he's
stretched a captain's armband around
his head.

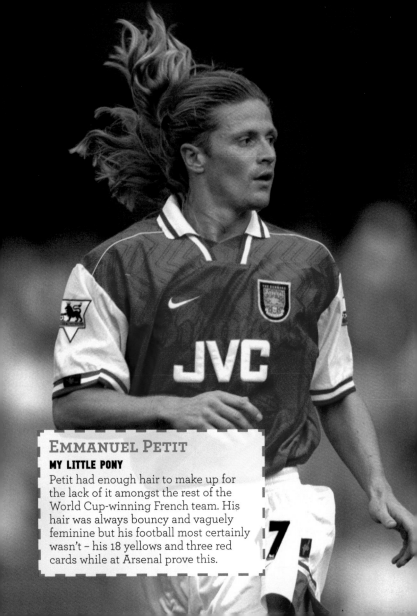

EMMANUEL PETIT

MY LITTLE PONY

Petit had enough hair to make up for the lack of it amongst the rest of the World Cup-winning French team. His hair was always bouncy and vaguely feminine but his football most certainly wasn't – his 18 yellows and three red cards while at Arsenal prove this.

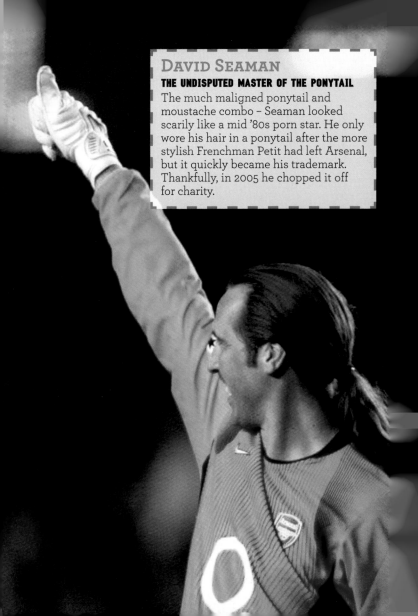

DAVID SEAMAN
THE UNDISPUTED MASTER OF THE PONYTAIL

The much maligned ponytail and moustache combo – Seaman looked scarily like a mid '80s porn star. He only wore his hair in a ponytail after the more stylish Frenchman Petit had left Arsenal, but it quickly became his trademark. Thankfully, in 2005 he chopped it off for charity.

HARRY KEWELL

PRAMFACE

Kewell's insistence on wearing his hair in a ponytail means we can't see if he's sporting the great Australian haircut – the 4'n'20. Instead his two or sometimes three ponytails give him a proper Croydon Facelift.

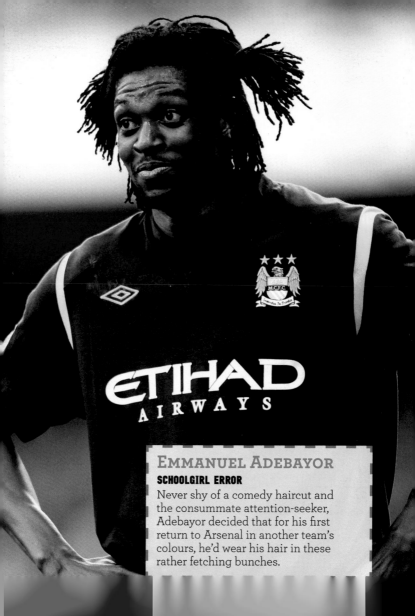

EMMANUEL ADEBAYOR

SCHOOLGIRL ERROR

Never shy of a comedy haircut and the consummate attention-seeker, Adebayor decided that for his first return to Arsenal in another team's colours, he'd wear his hair in these rather fetching bunches.

Braids & Afros

Twenty years ago there were no footballers with ribbons in their hair – now it doesn't raise an eyebrow. It's become part of the footballer's arsenal – braided hair is saying, 'Look at my hair not at the ball. Keep looking at my hair, look away from the ball. Look around the ball, look at those lovely coloured braids – now look – IT'S A GOAL.' It mesmerises an opponent and distracts him from getting a tackle in.

At least braids keep a player's hair in check. When combed free into an Afro it takes on a more laid back, party style. But it is useful on the football pitch – it makes a player taller so it's easier to head a ball and all that hair means

GERVINHO

NOT A BRAZILIAN

Part bald, part braid and
part headband, Gervinho
undoubtedly sported the star
haircut at the 2010 World
Cup. When Robbie Savage
says your hair is the worst
he's ever seen, you know
you're in trouble.

TARIBO WEST

TUNE IN

It's hard to say whether this even counts as hair. Antenna might be more accurate, but whatever you call it, West always matched it to the colour of his kit – that's dedication.

BACARY SAGNA

KEEP IT IN THE FAMILY

Sagna's beaded curtain hairstyle is the result of a boyhood bet
with his father. And believe it or not, he won. He was told he
could have his hair however he wanted if he scored in his next
game – which he duly did. Nowadays, his mother braids it for
him as it's too difficult to do himself.

COBI JONES

HAKUNA MATATA

Poster boy for USA 'soccer', Cobi Jones was like a lion prowling the midfield. Already one of the fastest players in MLS history, imagine how much quicker he'd have been if he'd not been carrying around the weight of all those dreads.

MAROUANE FELLAINI

CALM DOWN, CALM DOWN

Fellaini has undoubtedly got the biggest hair in the Premier League. However, rumours that he is taking traditional Scouse curly hair to new extremes have proved unfounded.

18

JÔ

BED HAIR IN EXTREMIS

João Alves de Assis Silva has the look of someone who spends most of his time asleep. Amazingly enough, his five clubs in five years are testament to the fact that he doesn't seem to settle anywhere.

RIO FERDINAND

WIIIIIIICCCCCKKKKKKEEEEEEEEEEED!

The four-times Premier League winning
Manchester United captain has always fancied
himself as a bit of a joker. And with this Afro he
sported in 2004 we can see why.

Mohicans

No hairstyle screams, 'Are you looking at me?' quite like the mohican, or mohawk. Originally worn by Native American warriors going off to fight, it is designed to intimidate and strike fear into your enemy. Adopted by punks in the '70s, it spoke of alienation and rebellion.

When first worn on the football pitch in 2001 by David Beckham (obviously), a few brave players followed. The World Cup in 2002 was the high point for the mohican but it was never as popular as other styles – perhaps because it was a little too attention-seeking.

Later we saw the rise of the faux-hawk – a style created for those wanting to look 'hard' but not quite tough enough to do it for real.

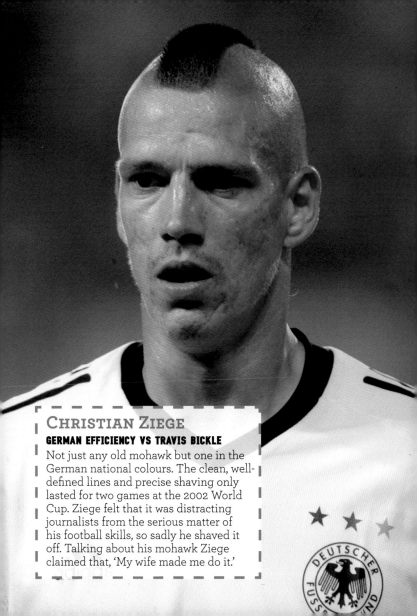

CHRISTIAN ZIEGE
GERMAN EFFICIENCY VS TRAVIS BICKLE

Not just any old mohawk but one in the German national colours. The clean, well-defined lines and precise shaving only lasted for two games at the 2002 World Cup. Ziege felt that it was distracting journalists from the serious matter of his football skills, so sadly he shaved it off. Talking about his mohawk Ziege claimed that, 'My wife made me do it.'

CLINT MATHIS

LAST OF THE MOHICANS

Mathis inflicted this punishment on
his head because he 'wanted to fit in
with the rest of the world'. Obviously
he doesn't get out much.

UMIT DAVALA

NICE BEAVER

Twice as wide as a regular mohican, Davala's crop is twice as bizarre. Never has a player made the simple look so difficult.

ALAN SMITH

WHY DOES IT ALWAYS RAIN ON ME?

Smith's hair is frustrating – it's trying
hard, all the skills are there but the final
product isn't what it should be. If he was
German he'd be a less skilful Bastian
Schweinsteiger.

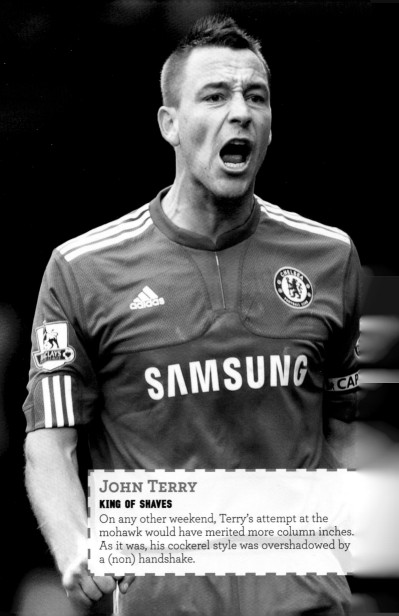

JOHN TERRY

KING OF SHAVES

On any other weekend, Terry's attempt at the
mohawk would have merited more column inches.
As it was, his cockerel style was overshadowed by
a (non) handshake.

KAZUYUKI TODA

PARROT FASHION

Japanese players dyed their hair red for the 2002 World Cup to allegedly attract European scouts. Toda went the extra yard and wore his hair in a mohawk. He ended up at Spurs – go figure.

MAREK HAMSIK

PRETTY VACANT

We're not sure what is Slovakian for 'Help, I've got my fingers stuck in a light socket' but Hamsik will be able to tell us. His goal celebration centres around preening his hair for which we can thank his punk stylist girlfriend, who created his strong look.

Shavers

A very modern phenomenon is the footballer's haircut that is shaved into increasingly bizarre patterns. There isn't one defining shaved haircut but there is one defining question – WHY?

Perhaps all those lines on a players head are a mobile tactics board for the team – telling a team mate which mazy run to make. Or maybe that bizarre thatch is a reminder that they are playing the Christmas tree formation.

From displays of patriotism to acts of fun it never looks the best. In fact, it often ends up looking like a player has been auditioning for a part in the next George Lucas movie. Either that or they've fallen asleep at the Christmas party and

Ronaldo

THE HAIRSTYLE WITH NO NAME

From the mohawk to the braids, there are plenty of hairstyles that make the transfer from player to public. We can safely say that this isn't one of them – it's almost half a haircut. Ronaldo said it was his way of dealing with the pressure on him during the 2002 World Cup, but it caused a fist fight to break out amongst the hordes of Brazilian journalists wanting to question him about it. It certainly didn't do him any harm – he scored both the goals in the final as Brazil beat Germany 2-0.

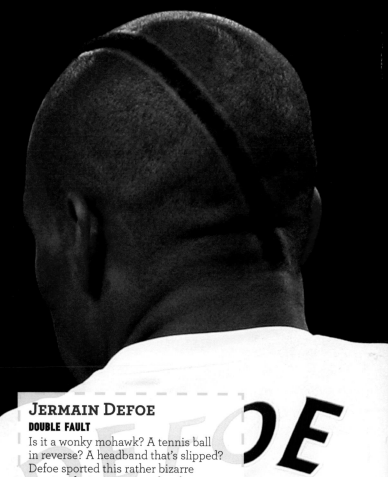

JERMAIN DEFOE
DOUBLE FAULT
Is it a wonky mohawk? A tennis ball in reverse? A headband that's slipped? Defoe sported this rather bizarre creation for just one match – the Carling Cup semi versus Arsenal at The Emirates. Despite the abuse he got from the home fans he had the last laugh as Spurs won the second leg 5-1.

AARON LENNON

SCREAM IF YOU WANT TO GO FASTER

Lennon is a player who certainly doesn't need go-faster stripes – he can run at over 20mph.

Loco

CRAZY HAIR IN ANY LANGUAGE

Manuel Cange's nickname couldn't be
more appropriate. He's the only player
ever to attempt Ronaldo's haircut –
putting spidery braids at the front to
add his own flourish to it. Unfortunately,
it's like putting a hat on the Mona Lisa –
you shouldn't mess with perfection.

STEVEN PIENAAR

SHORT FRONT AND SIDES

South Africa captain Pienaar's braids
make sense – they keep his long hair in
check. So, it's the shaved front and sides
that make Pienaar go from the almost
acceptable to the downright ridiculous.

PAUL JONES

'CAN I HAVE A NO. 50 PLEASE?'

When the Welsh goalkeeper reached 50 caps, he shaved a dragon on the back of his head and the number 50 onto both sides. But the Slovakia match was one to forget – he let in five goals – Wales' worst result for 98 years.

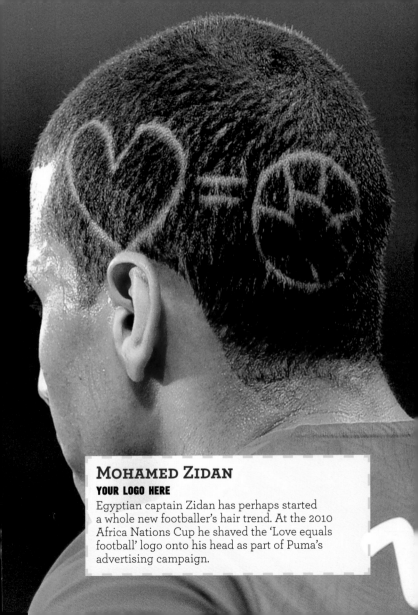

Mohamed Zidan

YOUR LOGO HERE

Egyptian captain Zidan has perhaps started
a whole new footballer's hair trend. At the 2010
Africa Nations Cup he shaved the 'Love equals
football' logo onto his head as part of Puma's
advertising campaign.

Baldies

These days you won't see any player sporting the Bobby Charlton comb-over – it's just not cool to try to hide the fact that you are going bald. Players now shave it all off as a fashion statement – they are bald and proud.

From those who are receding at the front to those that have a penalty spot on top, there's only one thing worth saying to their hair – 'You're off'.

Perhaps overzealous heading of the ball could be blamed, but certain positions seem to be balder than others. You only need to look at Heurelho Gomes and Pepe Reina in the Premier League to see that there's a disproportionate number of goalies with no hair. Is it to distract the striker into thinking their head is the ball?

FABIEN BARTHEZ

THE FRENCH BLARNEY STONE

Not the only bald goalkeeper – they are two-a-
penny. Not the only bald French World Cup winner
– step forward Mr Leboeuf. But Barthez is the only
player who's bald head was used as a good luck
charm. Laurent Blanc kissed it before each game –
but the luck ran out for Blanc who missed the 1998
World Cup final after being controversially sent off
in the semi.

WAYNE ROONEY

BOBBY CHARLTON'S HEIR

Wayne Rooney looked uncannily like
a grown man at 12 – still only 24, his
hair seems intent on making him look
older still.

STEVE BOULD

1–0 TO THE BARNET

It wouldn't have happened if his name was Steve Hirsute.

Pierluigi Collina

WHO LOVES YA, BABY?

Iconic. Not a footballer – but football
over the last 20 years wouldn't have
been the same without him. The best
and most distinctive referee – he should
be cloned so all refs look and officiate
like him. Perhaps he has, as Howard
Webb's distictive shiny dome officiated
the 2010 World Cup Final.

Borislav Mikhailov

BULGARIAN SYRUP

Mikhailov captained the great Bulgaria team of 1994, but he is best remembered for his wig – a first in football.

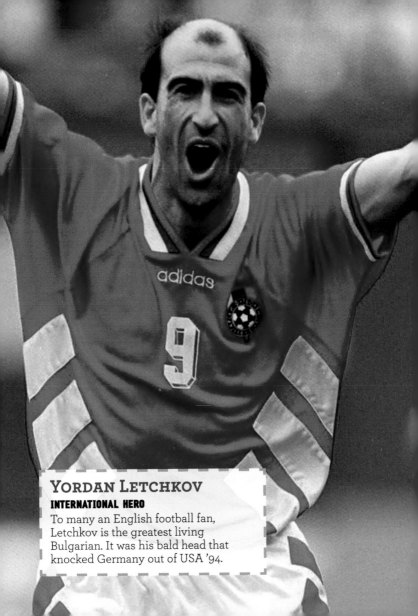

YORDAN LETCHKOV

INTERNATIONAL HERO

To many an English football fan, Letchkov is the greatest living Bulgarian. It was his bald head that knocked Germany out of USA '94.

ZINEDINE ZIDANE

SEE YOU, MARCO

Brooding and intense, monk-like and
serene. Maybe Zidane's hair knew that
his final act on the football pitch would
be to headbutt Marco Materazzi and
it didn't want to be there to see the
aftermath.

Beardies

For years a beard was a relatively uncommon sight on the football pitch. But recently they've been creeping back and they are a joy to behold.

Modern footballers' facial hair has tended to be more subtle – decorative and almost sculptural. The likes of Beckham and Carlos Cuellar show that there is a renaissance of the bushy 'George Best 1972' look. With players getting younger and younger, there's also an increase in the 'I've grown this wispy moustache so they'll serve me in the pub' look – as modelled by Theo Walcott.

Even with this newfound enthusiasm for facial hair, it will be a long while before we see the French Fork, the Hollywoodian or the Hulihee on the pitch – unless they become team formations.

GENNARO GATTUSO

A HEAD OF HIS TIME

There was a time when Gattuso was
the only top footballer with a beard. He
trimmed it when Milan were playing
well and let it get wild and scary when
they needed a result. A combative
midfielder, his no-nonsense facial hair
gives him the appearance of a gladiator
looking for his next kill.

ROBERT PIRES

ALL FOR ONE AND ONE FOR ALL
Pires perfected the musketeer look – the flowing locks and the interesting facial hair. 'The Pires' has even passed into urban language as a description for a thin line of pubic hair.

DAVID VILLA

KIND OF BLUE

Not the best Villa beard by a long
stretch – that would be Peter Withe
of the Aston Villa 1982 European Cup
winning team. In fact David Villa's soul
patch isn't really a proper beard at all
– it's more something a fifties jazz man
would grow to impress the ladies.

MAURICIO VICTORINO

CHINNY RECKON

Clearly in Uruguay, Jimmy Hill isn't a household name.

ALEXI LALAS

THE GENRE BUSTER, GENERAL CUSTER

He had everything. The Catweazle beard, the headband, the long flowing locks and he's got to be the gingerest footballer ever (sorry Scholesy). If footballers are the new rock stars then Alexi Lalas is The Grateful Dead.

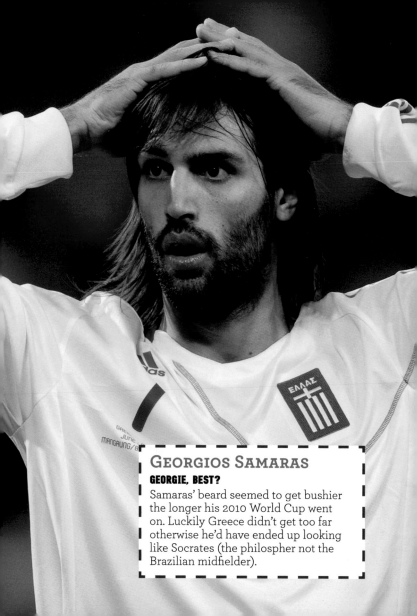

GEORGIOS SAMARAS

GEORGIE, BEST?

Samaras' beard seemed to get bushier the longer his 2010 World Cup went on. Luckily Greece didn't get too far otherwise he'd have ended up looking like Socrates (the philospher not the Brazilian midfielder).

RIGOBERT SONG

EBONY AND IVORY

It's the law that if you bleach your beard you must have a really serious facial expression so people think someone has played a prank on you. Otherwise, they may think that you chose to do it yourself.

Schoolboys

There are those whose hair never changes from their debut onwards. It's the same haircut that they've had since their schooldays – solid and dependable – something simple, functional and definitely not flashy.

It speaks of football being a priority not fashion – of sticking to what you know. Maybe they just play it safe because of the bewildering options available to them or perhaps their hair won't do anything else.

Then there are the schoolboy errors – when it all goes wrong with the addition of too much 'product' – the hair gel experiments and the timid use of highlights. What all these styles show is that 'mum knows best'.

PETER BEARDSLEY

MOTHER'S RUIN

Beardsley's hair looked like his mum
cut it using a breadknife, a basin and
a blindfold. With a name like that, the
very least we'd have expected was a bit
of facial hair.

RYAN GIGGS

SHAVING'S PRIVATE, RYAN

835 appearances, 152 goals, 30 medals
and after this youthful flat-top, only
one haircut. It has got greyer over
his 20-year playing career but Giggs
has kept his hair the same and let his
football do the talking.

PAUL SCHOLES

THE GINGER NINJA

Unchanged. His picture from the '94 Panini album is exactly the same as the one from 2010. Paul Scholes is the Anti-Beckham. Imagine him with a mohican. Or a skinhead. Or a ponytail. You just can't.

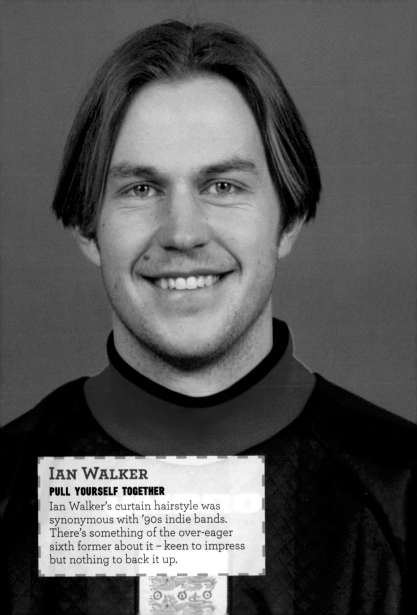

IAN WALKER

PULL YOURSELF TOGETHER

Ian Walker's curtain hairstyle was synonymous with '90s indie bands. There's something of the over-eager sixth former about it – keen to impress but nothing to back it up.

TEDDY SHERINGHAM
OH TEDDY, TEDDY
Sensible. Hair like a bank manager. Even after winning the Champions League there wasn't a hair out of place.

Tomás Rosicky

THERE'S SOMETHING ABOUT TOMAS

Has Rosicky applied a little too much wax or is he just pleased to see me?

CHRIS EAGLES

MAN, THE CROW'S NEST

His hair even has its own Facebook
fan page – 'Chris Eagles – the future of
English football and stylish hair'. Its 174
members can't be wrong, can they?

CRISTIANO RONALDO

CRISTIANO-NO

Pictured here aged 18, Ronaldo's hair
is fussy, over-tricksy and a little bit too
flashy. As he's matured, it's got simpler
and more direct, but the end result is
just as powerful.

TIMO KUNERT
A FLOCK OF SEAGULLS
Once in a while you see a haircut that defies explanation. Schalke midfielder Kunert's post -modern New Romantic barnet is one such moment.

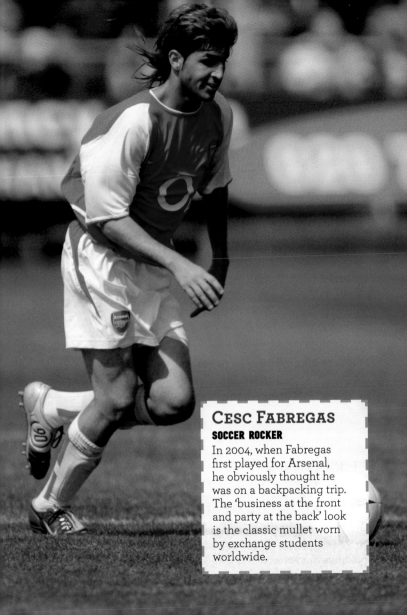

CESC FABREGAS
SOCCER ROCKER
In 2004, when Fabregas first played for Arsenal, he obviously thought he was on a backpacking trip. The 'business at the front and party at the back' look is the classic mullet worn by exchange students worldwide.

FERNANDO TORRES

POST-MULLET STRESS DISORDER

The rare sighting of highlights on a
footballer. Schoolboy error. Strangely
enough, Torres' new haircut was
blamed for his poor form at the 2010
World Cup – who'd have thought
that highlights like these could be
a postitive influence?

MILOS KRASIC
A SHOCK OF BLOND HAIR
It's a shame that Serbia didn't get out
of their group at the 2010 World Cup as
Krasic's all-natural hair was one of the
few truly unusual barnets on display in
South Africa.

LIONEL MESSI

LIONEL TIDY

The greatest player in the world has the sensiblest hairstyle in the world. He looks like he'd be more at home rounding up trolleys at Sainsbury's than dazzling the Nou Camp.

The Rainbow

Back in the '90s things were simple – just bleach your hair and the world would take notice. The Romania team at France '98 certainly took this to heart, but it had a negative effect on their football as they didn't win another game.

Nowadays players have to go the extra yard. There isn't a colour or pattern that hasn't been seen on the football pitch – and sometimes all at the same time.

There's always something of the attention-seeker about a player who dyes their hair, but does it cover up for a lack of inspiration elsewhere? Surely it's not a coincidence that no footballer with outrageously dyed hair has got a World Cup winner's medal.

PAUL GASCOIGNE

TAKE THAT AND PARTY

Euro '96 – Football's Coming Home, The Dentist's Chair celebration, penalty heartache (again) and Gazza's iconic blond crop. This hair was was the style of choice for footballers and pop stars alike. It's the haircut Gascoigne will be best remembered for, rather than the hair extensions he sported for one day before even he realised it was a bad idea.

ABEL XAVIER

THE FOOTBALLING NEPTUNE

Football needs players like Abel Xavier.
He serves to make most other players'
hair seem normal by comparison and
he's the prime example of a player
who will be remembered more for his
hairstyles than for his ability. And when
he played for LA Galaxy things got a
whole lot more bizarre (see front cover).

ROBBIE FOWLER

PARALLEL LINES

Never one to shy away from controversy, Fowler's bleached hair was probably the low point of his Anfield career – but at least he didn't have a Scouser bubble perm and 'tache.

FREDDIE LJUNGBERG

WE LOVE YOU, FREDDIE, BECAUSE YOU'VE GOT RED HAIR

Another player to style himself on a parakeet. The Arsenal fans sang songs about his red hair. He eventually shaved it off because he only trusted his barber back in Sweden to colour it for him and it became too difficult to travel there to get it done.

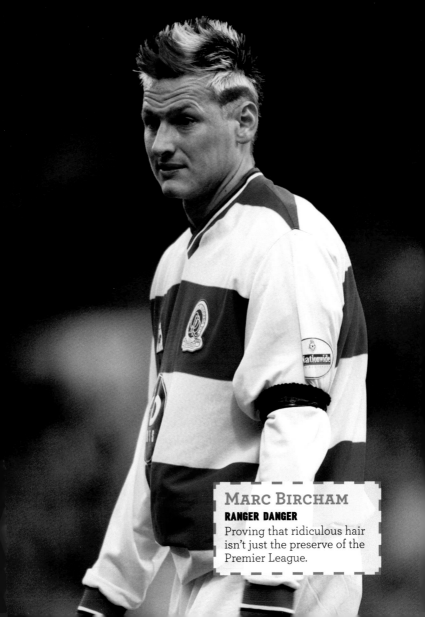

MARC BIRCHAM

RANGER DANGER

Proving that ridiculous hair isn't just the preserve of the Premier League.

PAUL SCHARNER

KEEP YOUR WIG ON

Scharner claimed to dye his hair to get some media attention – at least the hair distracted from his football skills. With this colour combination his team let in four against Everton. A half black and half white hairstyle didn't work either as Wigan conceded nine against Spurs.

IBRAHIMA SONKO

STARS IN HIS EYES

Sonko has played for many clubs in his short career, but the Vidal Sassoon Showbiz Eleven is not one of them.

Freestylers

Certain players deserve a lifetime achievement award for their services to football haircuts – they change their hair so often that it is hard to categorise them. They are not afraid to experiment and do so with wholehearted enthusiasm and joy.

David James epitomises this chameleon-like approach to the footballer's haircut. From Superman to Slim Shady, he'll try anything once. He once even claimed that his hair kept out a Michael Owen shot.

Flamboyant striker Djibril Cisse gets plenty of headlines for his hair and has inspired countless hair-related terrace chants.

It's safe to say that wherever they've played, our freestylers are definitely a cut above the rest.

2009

2003

2004

2006

2007

2003   2003

2008   2008